Little Hackers

When Grandpa's computer falls victim to malware, it's up to Zuri to save the day! Using an engaging story with beautiful illustrations, this picture book makes it easy to introduce your child or student to basic computer science concepts and vocabulary. While being entertained, children will learn the difference between black, white, and gray hat hackers, how to identify malware, how to create secure passwords, and more!

Embark on a delightful exploration of computer science and ethical hacking concepts through the eyes of a precocious young child!

Consider the companion guidebook *Supporting the Development of Computer Science Concepts in Early Childhood* to help dig even deeper, engender excitement, and provide a solid understanding of computer science that sets your learner up for success!

For effective use, this book should be purchased alongside the guidebook. The guidebook, *Little Hackers,* and an additional storybook, *Little Computer Scientists*, can be purchased together as a set, *Developing Computer Science Concepts in Early Childhood* [978-1-032-47108-2].

Julie Darling is a teacher/librarian at the Ann Arbor STEAM school. She has a Master of Science in Information from the University of Michigan and is a Raspberry Pi certified educator. Julie has been teaching technology for more than 20 years.

D. J. Cools is a writer, illustrator, and designer with a passion for books, outdoor adventure, and old cars. Originally from Washington State, D. J. enjoys cycling, exploring, and small-town family life in Southeastern Michigan.

T0314546

Little Hackers

Written by

Julie Darling

Illustrated by

D. J. Cools

First published 2025
by Routledge
605 Third Avenue, New York, NY 10158

and by Routledge
4 Park Square, Milton Park, Abingdon, Oxon, OX14 4RN

Routledge is an imprint of the Taylor & Francis Group, an informa business

Library of Congress Cataloging-in-Publication Data
Names: Darling, Julie, author. | Cools, Darren, illustrator.
Title: Little hackers / Julie Darling; illustrated by Darren Cools.
Other titles: Little hacker
Description: New York: Routledge, 2024. | For effective use, this book should be purchased alongside the guidebook Little Hackers, and an additional storybook, Little Computer Scientists, can be purchased together as a set, Developing Computer Science Concepts in Early Childhood. | Audience: Ages 5+ | Audience: Grades 2-3
Identifiers: LCCN 2024015933 (print) | LCCN 2024015934 (ebook) | ISBN 9781032471143 (pbk) | ISBN 9781003501527 (ebk)
Subjects: LCSH: Computer security–Juvenile literature. | Hacking–Juvenile literature. | Malware (Computer software)–Juvenile literature.
Classification: LCC QA76.9.A25 D337 2024 (print) | LCC QA76.9.A25 (ebook) | DDC 005.8/7–dc23/eng/20240522
LC record available at https://lccn.loc.gov/2024015933
LC ebook record available at https://lccn.loc.gov/2024015934

ISBN: 978-1-032-47114-3 (pbk)
ISBN: 978-1-003-50152-7 (ebk)

DOI: 10.4324/9781003501527

Typeset in Calibri
by Deanta Global Publishing Services, Chennai, India

Dear readers—sometimes you need to try on different hats. It's important to know which to wear, and when to wear it.

—Julie Darling

For Darrell and Dann, who introduced me to the magic of computers.

—D. J. Cools

Zuri tries on her **black hat**.

She tries on her **gray hat**.

She decides to wear her **white hat** today.

She checks in with Grandpa
to see how he's doing.

What's that on his
computer display?

Oh no! It's a **pop-up ad.**

His computer's running slowly.

It's been crashing *all day.*

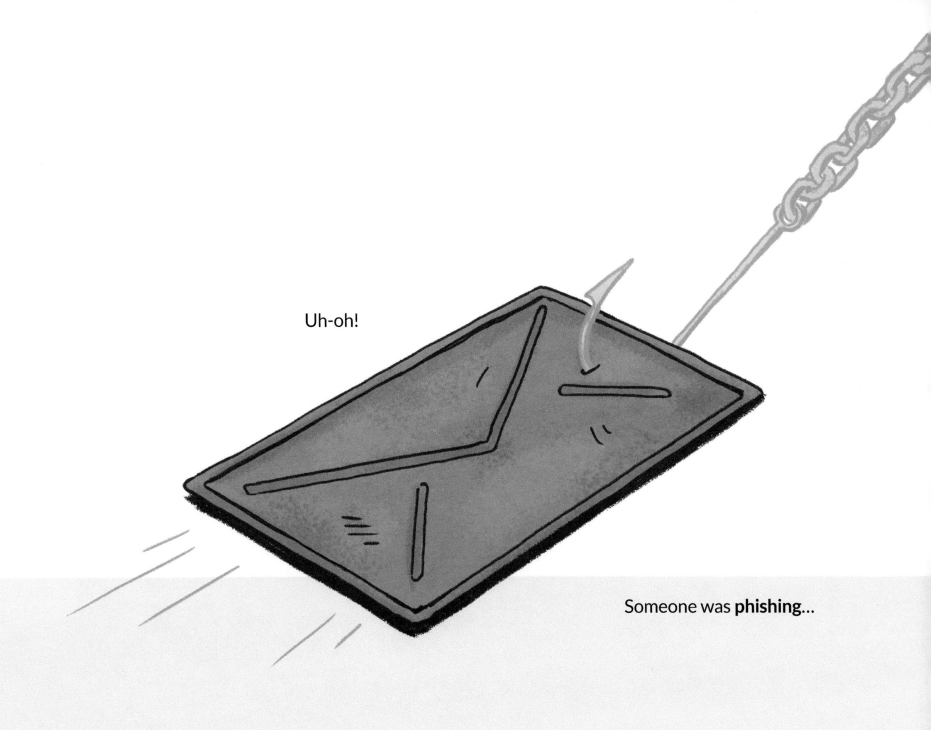

Uh-oh!

Someone was **phishing**...

Grandpa downloaded **malware.**

How do we make it go away?

Zuri calls on her friends.

They all **Zoom** in to fix the problem.

The Little Hackers are here to save the day!

They install a **virus scanner** and reboot into **safe-mode**.

The virus is now **quarantined**—hooray!

But Grandpa's not safe yet...

They need to change the **password**.

A new, more secure one. Without delay.

They know to make it long.

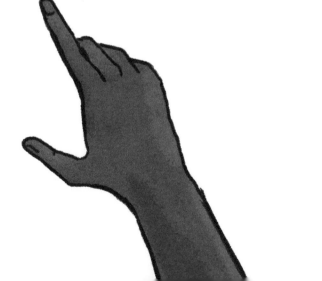

Add symbols and capital letters.

Zuri makes sure Grandpa won't forget it,
teaches him to be more careful.

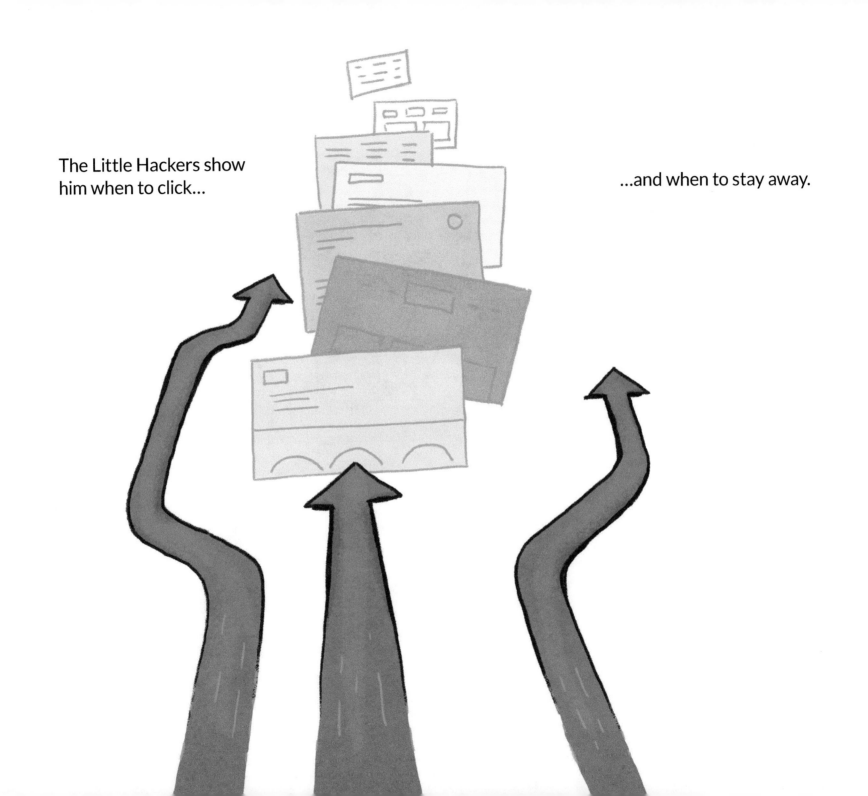

Now Grandpa's safe from **malware**.

No **Trojan Horse** can trick him.

Everyone's free to code
and hack and play.

But wait! Where are the cookies?

They were freshly
baked and waiting.

Zuri puts on her gray hat with dismay!

She hacks her sister's camera.

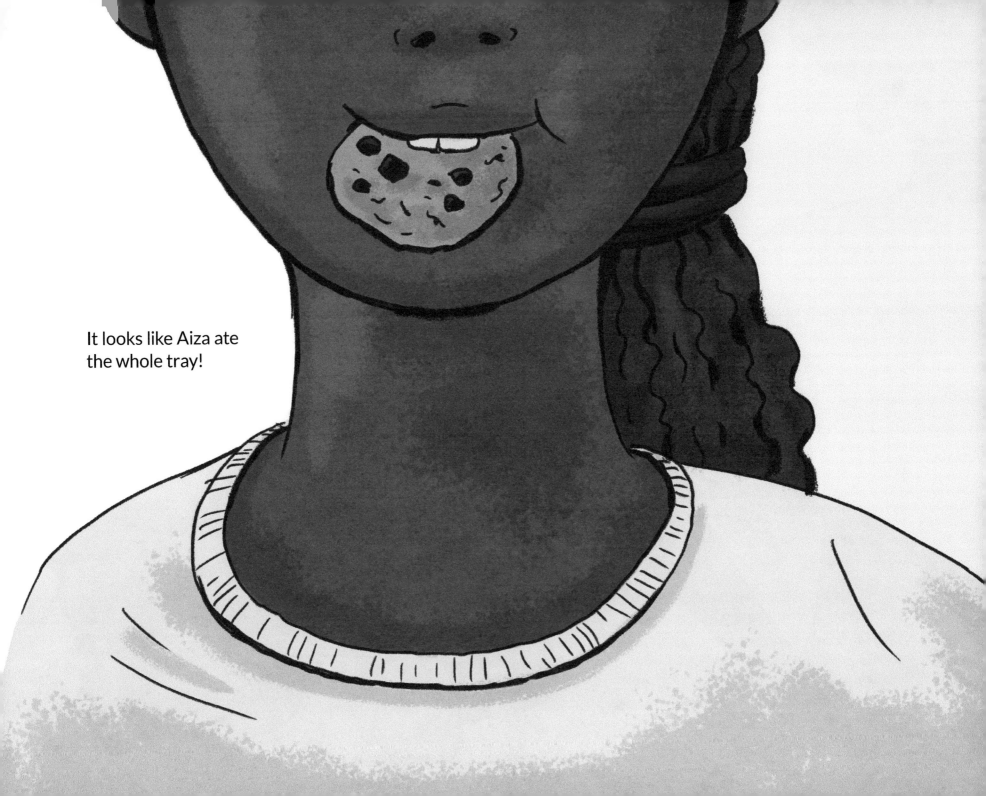

It looks like Aiza ate
the whole tray!

Zuri storms into her room, only to find Aiza laughing.

She tricked her—
there's a fake picture
(of cookie crumbs)
positioned in
the way.

There are still cookies for everyone!

Warm and gooey from the oven.

A nice reward for working hard today.

Author's Note

Kids given exposure to pertinent vocabulary and essential concepts in any field of study are more likely to have success (and are more likely to be interested) in that discipline. This book (and its companion—*Little Computer Scientists*) aims to do just that.

Here are more details about the vocabulary and concepts explored in this story.

Hackers aren't always up to no good. There are three categories of hacking: white hat, gray hat, and black hat. **White hat** hacking is what cybersecurity experts do. They work to find and fix vulnerabilities and try to prevent other hackers from getting in. **Gray hat** hacking is when someone hacks into systems (without permission) in order to raise awareness and expose vulnerabilities. **Black hat** hacking is when someone hacks into a system (without permission) with the intent to do damage and/or steal information.

Pop-ups are advertisements (and other messages) that pop up on your screen. Sometimes they're simply advertisements. However, one type of black hat hacking is to create a pop-up ad that tells users they have a virus on their computer and that they need to download software to clean the system. However, when they download that software, instead of cleaning the system, it installs a virus. Another common tactic is not to install a virus, but to tell the user the device is infected with malware and instruct the user to call a telephone number that the scammer answers. Then s/he will trick the user into installing software that allows the scammer to control the user's device. Lots of pop-ups suddenly appearing is often a sign that there is malware installed on your computer. When your computer is suddenly running more slowly than usual, that can also be indicative of malware.

Phishing is when someone tries to trick you into giving them your information. Phishing scams are used to steal anything from passwords to bank account information. One of the most common types of phishing is to send an email that asks you to click on a link, to log into an external account. Once you click on that link, a fake account login page is opened, and you unknowingly input your login credentials into a login page that the scammer controls. Now the scammer has your credentials and account information.

Malware, also called malicious software, is a program that's designed to cause harm. Different types of malware do different things, including: slowing down your device, sending spam emails that infect other devices (viruses), stealing your personal data, or even preventing you from accessing anything on your device until you pay the hacker money (ransomware).

Zoom is cloud-based video conferencing software used to connect with video, audio, chat, and screen-sharing.

Virus scanners are part of antivirus software. When you run antivirus software, it searches through your system to locate and remove malware.

To **reboot** using **safe-mode** means that you restart the computer in such a way that you're only running the most basic programs your computer needs to run. This way of restarting your device helps you to identify and fix potential problems (including malware and viruses).

A **quarantined virus** is a virus that has been confined to a safe area where it can't infect the rest of your device. You do this using anti-virus software.

A **secure password** is a password that is long (the longer the better) and contains a combination of letters (capital and lower-case), numbers, and symbols. In addition, your password is much more secure if unique passwords are used for each account (or credential). Also, you should avoid using easily guessable information such as birth dates, family or pet names, the word "password", or really any word(s) found in a dictionary. Finally, consider using multi-factor authentication for additional security.

An example of a **brute-force attack** is when a hacker attempts to gain access to your account by trying every possible password combination. If your password is short (e.g., a four-digit number) or a word found in a dictionary, it's more vulnerable to brute-force attacks.

A **Trojan Horse**, named after the ancient Greek story about the fall of the city of Troy, is when malware is disguised as a legitimate program. Once downloaded, the malware causes harm.

If you'd like more resources for teaching your littles the basics of computer science, consider pairing *Little Hackers* with *Little Computer Scientists* and *Supporting the Development of Computer Science Concepts in Early Childhood: A Practical Guide for Parents and Educators*. Together, these books will help you to give your little ones a solid foundational knowledge base for understanding and excelling at computer science.